Sea and Cedar

Sea and Cedar

How the Northwest Coast Indians Lived

By Lois McConkey

Illustrations by Douglas Tait

J.J. Douglas Ltd.
Vancouver, 1973

ISBN 0-88894-042-4

73 74 75 76 77 5 4 3 2 1

J.J. Douglas Ltd.
3645 McKechnie Avenue
West Vancouver, British Columbia

Designed by Jim Rimmer
Typesetting by Photype Centre Ltd.
Printed in Canada by Brock Webber Printing Company Ltd.

Contents

For Gordon, Mark and Karen

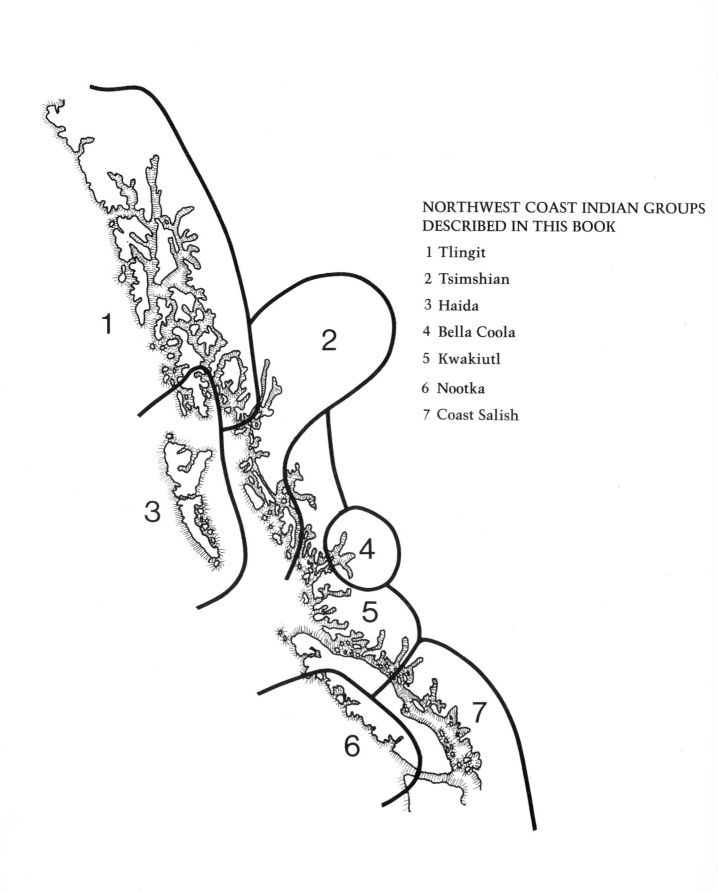

NORTHWEST COAST INDIAN GROUPS
DESCRIBED IN THIS BOOK

1 Tlingit

2 Tsimshian

3 Haida

4 Bella Coola

5 Kwakiutl

6 Nootka

7 Coast Salish

The Northwest Coast Indians
Introduction

When we think of an Indian, we usually imagine a
noble looking, dark skinned man, astride a pony,
with only a blanket for a saddle. Perhaps he is
chasing a herd of buffalo, or leading a group of
braves towards a cluster of teepees.
Such Indians did live in North America and there
have been movies and stories about them.
They lived on the prairies. But not all Indians lived
as those on the prairies did.

This book is a simple introduction to the
Northwest Coast Indians. They did not ride horses,
chase buffalo or live in teepees. Their fascinating
way of life was centered around the Pacific Ocean
and a tree: the cedar tree.

KWAKIUTL DANCERS

Canoes

The Northwest Coast Indians described in this book lived along the shores of Canada and the nearby shores of the United States, on the Pacific Ocean. They were isolated because of the high mountains to the east and the vast Pacific Ocean to the west.

The warm Japanese Current flows from Japan, curves around by Alaska, then flows down the Canadian shoreline, making the climate mild and wet. The warm air above the Japanese Current is stopped by the high mountains, causing the cold moisture in the air to turn to rain. Rain helps to produce masses of green growth: trees, shrubs, berry bushes and all kinds of plants, and on the Northwest Coast the tall tree with a thick gnarled bark called cedar.

JAPANESE CURRENT

NORTHERN CANOE

The Indians could make almost everything they needed from this tree including their homes, baskets, mats, ropes, spoons, dishes, totem poles and even their clothing.

Fish was a major food and source of oil so they needed boats, and from the cedar tree they made their canoes — big ones that would be paddled far out to sea.

First they had to find the right cedar tree. It had to be tall enough to make a canoe that would hold many men. Then they had to cut the large tree down without the saw or the axe that we have today, but with only stone hammers and sharp stone chisels.

At times the Indians hollowed out an opening at the base of a suitable tree in which they laid a fire. They used wet sand to guide the fire through the bottom of the tree and to prevent it from burning up the side.

The fire was started by rotating a pointed stick between their hands, causing the point of the stick to turn in a hole in a piece of soft wood surrounded by dry shredded cedar bark. Soon a spark would start a tiny flame, which was quickly fed with more bark, until a larger fire was burning.

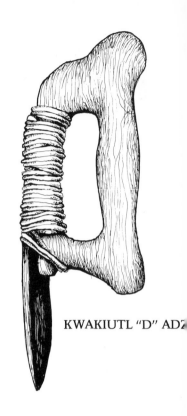

KWAKIUTL "D" ADZE

Some groups made a tool called a "D-adze". It was carved from wood and was shaped like our letter D. Something sharp was needed for a blade and as they had scarcely any metal, a flat hard stone could be sharpened for this purpose.

Others used an "elbow adze", which had a long handle that looked much like an elbow, with a sharp stone bound on the end with rope — again often made from cedar.

When the tree was on the ground, they shaped it with their adzes, stone hammers and chisels on the outside, and burned the center of the log with fire. Gradually, a large hole would be made and with much time and work the log would be hollowed out. Now the shape of the canoe had to be finished. They filled the hole with hot water, because in the same way that macaroni is made soft by dropping it into boiling water, wood when it is soaked in boiling water becomes soft and can then be shaped. But the Indians did not have pots or pans to boil water; they did make baskets that were woven so tightly that they could hold water without leaking, but of course the baskets would burn if held over a fire.

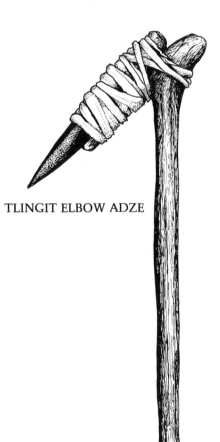

TLINGIT ELBOW ADZE

So they filled the canoe with cold water from the ocean. Close by, they built a fire and put large rocks into it until they were red hot. With long sticks they would lift the hot rocks into the canoe until the water became boiling hot. When the wood became soft, they put cross pieces in the canoe to shape the sides wider in the middle and more narrow at the ends. After the water was dumped out

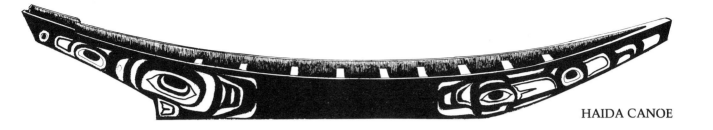

HAIDA CANOE

of the canoe, and the wood had cooled, it would keep its shape. Often bow and stern pieces were attached with such skill that the joins were difficult to see.

Now they would make the canoe as smooth as possible. Today we would use sandpaper, but they used the rough skin of the dogfish, an ugly little shark whose skin makes perfect sandpaper when it is dry.

With the canoe finished, it was greased with whale oil to help preserve it, and perhaps a design was carved on its bow. The Indians would take very good care of their canoe and never drag it across rocks, but would carry it, or make a path of brush and leaves to skid it over. They would cover it with cedar bark mats to keep it dry when they were not using it.

Canoes varied in size and shape, from small fishing craft to large canoes that could hold thirty people or more. These were used for long voyages or raiding parties on enemy tribes.

Paddles were sometimes made with a notch on the end to catch a tree or root and so keep the canoe steady or hold it off the rocks. Other paddles were long and pointed at the end, to enable the Indian to paddle silently when fishing.

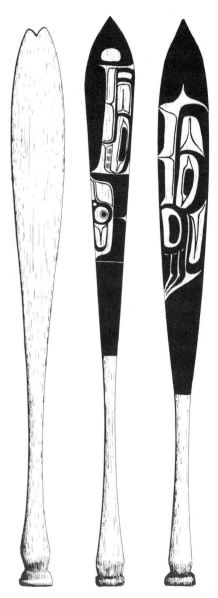

COAST SALISH
HAIDA PADDLE
TSIMSHIAN DESIGN ON PADDLE

Housing

The Northwest Coast Indians were not able to live in skin tents, because the climate was so wet. Such tents, after heavy rain, would become hard and brittle and would crack in the sun, just as leather shoes become hard and cracked after being soaked.

The Indians built houses made of wood, consisting of one very large room.

The four corner posts would be large tree trunks set in deep holes in the ground. It would take many men with strong ropes to pull the corner posts into

HAIDA HOUSE

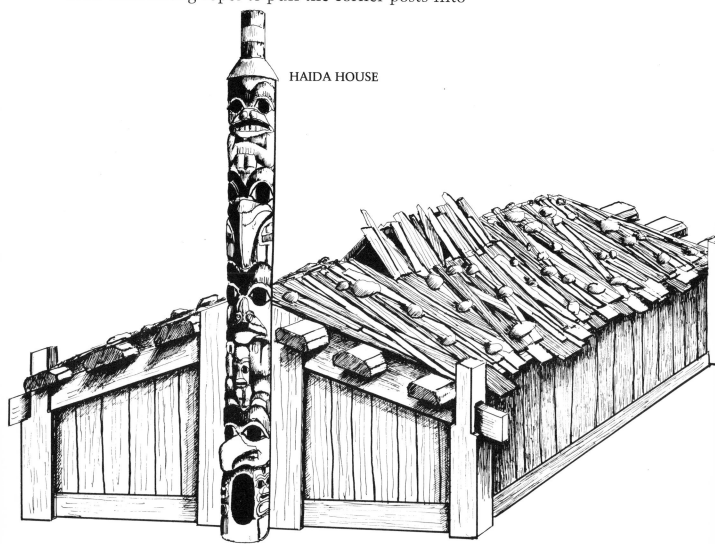

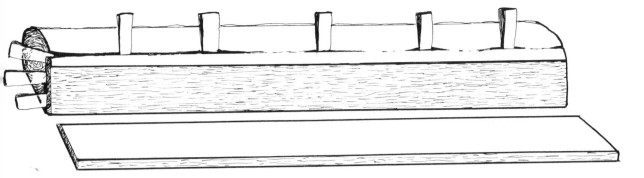

place. The walls were made of cedar planks. To make the planks, they pounded wedges, which are sharp pieces of wood, into the cedar log with a stone hammer, called a "maul," until the cedar log split into long planks.

The roof of the wooden house was made of cedar bark and planks, overlapping one another and held down with rocks. Roof lines and wall structure varied in different areas. At times the planks forming the walls were lashed and fitted separately, so that they could be taken down easily and moved to another frame at a fishing camp for the summer season.

There were no windows and only one small opening for an entrance. This helped keep the house warm. Some had a carved pole, called a house–frontal pole at the front. A hole was made in the house pole which made a doorway to the home.

Inside the house, along the walls, each family had its own living quarters. Cedar or bullrush mats were woven for partitions and walls. Each partition opened to the center of the house, where the fires were kept burning for heat, light and cooking. An opening in the center of the roof allowed the smoke to escape. Many families lived in one house, perhaps forty or sixty people, depending upon the size of the house. Although many related families lived in one house, each lived as a separate family and cooked its own meals, wove its own baskets and made its own clothing. In the summer the families set up camp near their fishing grounds or berry-picking territories.

HAIDA FRONTAL POLE

Food

It is not hard to imagine what Northwest Coast Indians ate. The Pacific Ocean was their great food basket as well as their highway, and salmon was their main food. Before the white settlers came, there were many salmon along the coast. The Indians would catch a lot when the fish came swimming up the rivers to lay their eggs. When they hatch, the small salmon swim downstream to the ocean to grow. When they are fully grown they swim up the freshwater streams to the lakes again to lay eggs, and the whole cycle starts again.

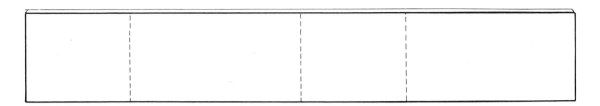

The Indians caught great numbers of salmon at the mouths of the streams during the salmon run. Then they had the problem of storing the salmon so that it would keep all year. They could not freeze it, because the climate was not cold enough, so they smoked it. They would hang the salmon over their fires and the smoke would preserve the fish and prevent it from decaying. Or they would dry it in the sun and wind.

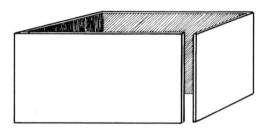

Boxes were also made that could hold water. They were called "bent boxes" or "property boxes," and were used for cooking or storing possessions. The Indians used one long piece of wood and made three grooves in it, then steamed the grooves until the wood became soft.

Then they bent it on the grooves to form four sides. They would fasten the two ends tightly together with lacing or tiny wooden pegs, then snugly fit a grooved bottom on it. Food was cooked by filling a box with water and adding hot rocks until the water was boiling.

HAIDA BENT BOX

The property boxes were often decorated with attractive carvings.

Other ways of preparing their food were by roasting over an open fire, or cooking in a large pit dug in the ground that worked just like an oven. Very hot rocks were placed in a hole in the ground and the food, wrapped in leaves, was placed on top. When hot rocks and earth covered the hole, the oven was ready. If the Indians wanted to steam their food, they sprinkled water on the rocks, or used a piece of kelp as a tube to the oven, and added water while the food was cooking.

The ocean produced other food: halibut, herring, cod, crabs, oysters, clams, mussels, sea weed and a great delicacy, fish eggs.

The Indians picked berries every year: cranberries, huckleberries, salalberries — many of the berries that we pick in the summer season today. They had to find a way to keep the berries from being spoiled. Today we preserve them in sugar; the Indians did not have sugar but often stored them in oil. They obtained oil from whales, seals, and from the eulachon fish, often storing it in bottles made from dried kelp. The eulachon fish was so oily that a cedar wick threaded through its body would make a fine candle, and it was sometimes called the "candle fish."

They also dried berries to keep them, just as we dry grapes and store the resulting raisins. Berries were also cooked to a thick mass, then dried in square boxes to form cakes.

And there was ample wild game for their diet, and birds. Usually they found it easier to catch their dinner in the ocean. Various roots, green shoots and the bark of certain trees where all prepared for eating.

The Nootka Indians, who lived on Vancouver Island, were the whale hunters of the Pacific Coast. They used the whale mostly for oil.

Only the Nootka Indian Chiefs had enough wealth to outfit the whaling canoes with their six well trained paddlers, a steersman and a chief, who was the harpooner. One canoe would paddle close to the whale so that it could be harpooned by the chief standing in the bow. Hunters, close by in

other boats, would plunge more harpoons into the whale. Seal skins, filled with air, were attached to the harpoon lines to slow the progress of the whale and aid the steersman in following it. When the whale was dead, its huge mouth was tied shut to prevent the whale from filling with water and sinking. Then began the long hard tow back to the village where they would be met with a great deal of ceremony.

Clothing

Clothing was made from the bark of the cedar tree: not the hard gnarled bark on the outside of the trunk, but the soft thin bark underneath. Care was taken not to strip too much bark from the tree, for that would kill it. The Indians were more concerned about conserving nature's gifts than the settlers who followed them. The Indians believed that the fish, birds, animals and the cedar tree were spirits. If they took more than was needed the spirits would be unhappy and punish them.

A section of the outer bark was carefully taken from the cedar tree, and the soft inner bark cut in long strips, rolled and taken back to the village. The yellow cedar bark was soaked in cold and then hot water until it was soft, then beaten with a "bark beater." This was usually made from whale bone. It had a handle and long grooves cut along the head.

When the bark had been beaten to soft shreds, it could be rolled between the palms of the hands and the upper leg, until it was the right thickness for weaving. The red cedar bark was not soaked, but split when dry, then twisted or shredded until it was soft.

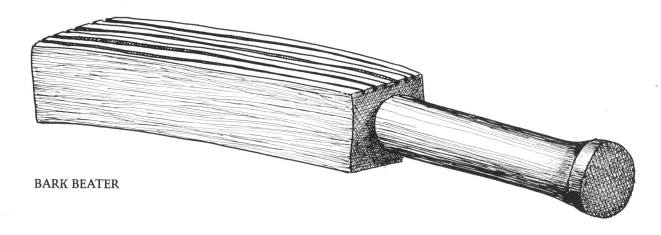

BARK BEATER

HAIDA DRESSED IN CEDAR BARK

To make a cedar bark cape, the strands of bark were woven in such a clever way that the fabric was water repellent. To make it softer around the neck, the Indians used fur, or wove in goat's hair or bird's down. The cape was made with a hole for the head, and hung over the shoulders. Skirts were made the same way. Rainproof hats were woven from spruce roots that had been heated, soaked and split. Sometimes they wove a design on the hat, representing an animal or bird.

HAIDA SPRUCE ROOT HAT

They also made a beautiful cape that we call a "Chilkat Blanket" which was worn only by a chief or a person of very high rank in the village. It was made from cedar bark and mountain goat hair. The Chilkat Blanket was woven with a design depicting an animal, bird or fish. It had a long fringe around

**CHILKAT BLANKET
(TLINGIT)**

the bottom. Decorated dance skirts were made in the same way, with highly prized dentalia shells trimming the bottom. They jingled when the Indian danced or walked. Robes of sea otter and other furs were also worn by people of high rank.

The hair of a white woolly dog was used by the Coast Salish Indians in their blanket weaving. This breed of dog was kept specially for this purpose.

The problem of foot covering was solved in the simplest manner. Skins would have become hard and brittle from the constant dampness and cedar bark shoes would soon be cut to ribbons with the rocky shores, so they usually went barefooted.

The Coastal Indian Chiefs did not wear feather head-dresses as the prairie Indians did. They wore a head-piece of carved wood, with tails of ermine hanging from it, and abalone shells fitted into the wooden carved area. Sea lion whiskers formed a circle around the top. This space could be filled

with bird's down which, during a ceremonial dance,
would flutter to the ground like snow.

A number of Indians living along the west
coast of Canada tattooed their bodies with their
crest designs. Women occasionally used labrets, a
carved piece of bone or stone that was placed
through the lower lip. Some of the coastal Indians
wrapped their babies' heads with cedar bark cloth,
and as the baby grew his forehead was forced into
a flat shape which was considered to be attractive.

TLINGIT CHIEF'S HEAD DRESS

Tools

STONE HAMMER

The Indians made their tools from anything they could find. As well as the D-adze, the elbow adze, and the wedge, a hammer (or maul) was made from stone. It looked like an old fashioned telephone receiver, and must have taken a lot of time to shape.

For a drill, they used a bone ground to a fine point inserted and tied on to a wooden shaft with cedar twine.

This was rotated between the palms of the hands so that the sharp point drilled a hole.

Chisels were made with a sharpened stone or a piece of horn set and tied to a wooden shaft.

Heavy stone mauls were made by some groups by securing a large shaped stone to a wooden shaft.

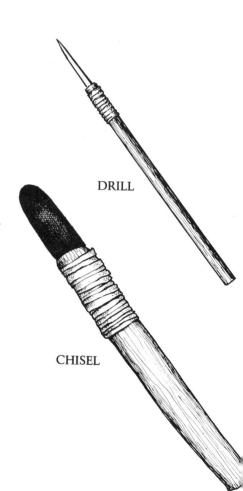

DRILL

CHISEL

HAIDA STONE MAUL

SEAL HARPOON HEAD

Hooks for catching fish were made, some from a spruce root that had been steamed and bent in the shape of a giant hair pin so that it would spring together on the open ends, like a lady's hair pin. The Indians would tie the fish bait behind the bone barb and put a stick in the end to hold the top and bottom apart. When the big fish went after the bait, his snout would knock the stick out of place and the top and bottom would snap together, forcing the bone spike into the head of the fish.

They had large harpoons for catching whales and seals, and smaller ones for salmon. They were made in sections and tied together to avoid losing the fish as well as the fishing equipment, which took a long time to make. Nets and traps for catching fish were also widely used.

SALMON HOOK — TLINGIT

HALIBUT HOOK

BLACK COD HOOK

TLINGIT HALIBUT HOOK

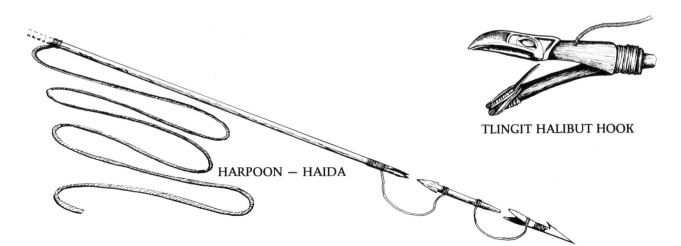

HARPOON — HAIDA

Potlatch

A "Potlatch" was a very important event: for a large one a chief may have invited many neighbouring tribes, perhaps five hundred people or more.

A potlach could be held to announce an important event, to give crests and titles to a new chief, to announce the marriage of a person of high rank, or to celebrate a new house or the raising of a new totem pole.

The people in the village would spend many months preparing. Food would have to be provided for all the guests. Gifts were made to be given away and masks made or repaired for the dances and songs.

Potlatches were important, as family rights and privileges of guests were announced and reminders made of each group's hunting and fishing territories. These formal announcements saved misunderstandings, and accomplished what our newspapers do today. The Indians had personal songs and dances which represented their family history and these were performed at the potlatch with appropriate family masks and with a great deal of drama. It was a fascinating way for the children to learn their family history.

The potlatch bowls that were made to serve the food were very large, almost the size of a small canoe, and the potlatch ladles or spoons were as big as footballs. The people would gather more food than could be eaten and have more gifts to give away than they had received at the previous potlatch.

The Northwest Coast Indian believed that having wealth and property was most important, and made the rest of the Indians respect and look up to him as a great man. He retained high rank and honour because he was able to give things away. The Indian did not have money: his wealth lay in his canoes, blankets, salves, masks, metal, dentalia shells, ermine skins and other possessions. Sheets of copper were highly prized, and to own one, break it or give it away, gave great respect to the owner. Rights to fishing areas and berry picking grounds, and ownership of titles, crests, songs and dances were also considered wealth.

COPPER —BASED ON HAIDA

HAIDA RATTLE

KWAKIUTL
WHISTLE

It took such a long time to gather enough property to give a big potlatch that they could not be held often, but they were necessary to enable a chief to pass on his wealth, and to maintain his rank and status.

For music, they made drums from planks placed on two wooden blocks. Drumsticks were made of wood. Tambourines were made with rawhide stretched over a hoop. Rattles, some beautifully carved, were made from wood, with pebbles or shells inside. They also made a bullroarer, which was a flat stick whirled on the end of a rope. Whistles were made from wood. A deer hoof rattle was made with hooves of deer tied to a long stick that was shaken up and down.

Beliefs

The Northwest Coast Indians believed that each person had a soul which became a ghost after death. Loss of a soul meant certain death, so it had to be found and recaptured. They also believed that it was possible to have a guardian spirit, which they had to seek for themselves, some without success.

Their doctors or medicine men were called "Shamans" and they were shown respect because they had the power to heal, and were able to recapture lost souls or drive out ghosts. This was done with a great deal of ceremony, using songs, rattles, drums and masks, and a carved tube of wood or bone that was open at both ends, called a "soul catcher."

They also believed that the dead were still with them in spirit form. They did not often bury the dead but would put them high up in a tree, or if they were important enough, build a totem pole for them and place them near the top on an especially carved piece of wood. Often they built a "burial house" in which they placed the bodies of their dead.

SOUL CATCHER

Art

EYE

SPLIT "U" FORM

HAND

CLAW

Indian carvings look much different from other art forms and perhaps they look a little confusing and strange. One form repeats itself very often: it is an ovoid form and can be used to make an eye.

Another form that is often used looks like a U.

The artists used these basic forms to carve or paint their legendary animals and birds. Often they would split their designs into many parts and add "ovoid" or "U" forms to fill in an empty space. This makes their artwork complicated and difficult to understand. We are just beginning to discover the advanced thinking that was represented by some great Indian artists.

They carved wooden columns of animal, bird and human figures. Some of these figures or symbols have definite features that help us to recognize them.

The bear has a short snout, large teeth, a tongue that slides out and large paws and claws.

HAIDA BEAR

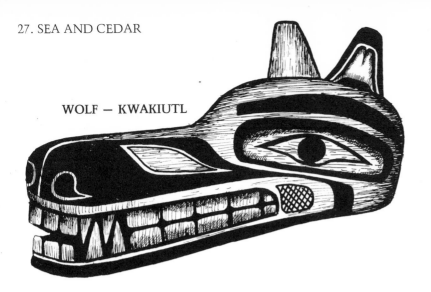

WOLF — KWAKIUTL

The wolf has a long nose and large teeth.

The beaver with a wide cross hatched tail is holding a stick between his paws, and has two large front incisors or teeth.

The killer whale has a long fin along his back and a large mouth.

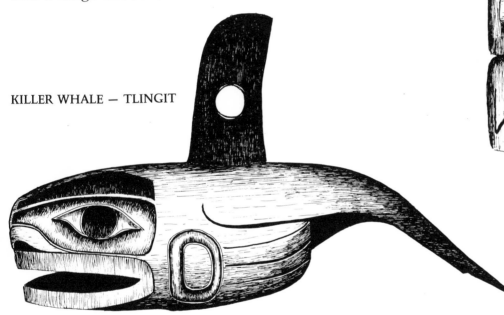

KILLER WHALE — TLINGIT

BEAVER — HAIDA

The raven always has a long straight beak and the eagle a beak that is curved down.

There were many other mythical figures that were used.

Although you may look at a totem pole and have an idea what image the Indian had carved, you may still not know the story it has to tell or what it represents. A knowledge of the Indian history, legend or myth that the artist was carving

RAVEN — TLINGIT

would be needed as well. The Indians used the animal and bird figures as symbols or crests to represent their family or group. There are many Indian legends and myths about the raven, wolf, beaver and other animals and birds.

Carved poles were erected for many reasons: They were made as a monument to a chief, or as a grave post for a person of high rank. The house front poles were placed against the wooden houses and an opening carved in the bottom to form the doorway. Carved poles were also used in the interior construction of the wooden houses as a means of support.

Totem poles were occasionally painted. Colors were made from bark, coals and burnt sea shells and then mixed with salmon eggs, and they were applied with brushes made from animal hair.

Arrival of the Explorers

Captain Cook, in 1778, was the first Englishman to land on Pacific Northwest shores. He was followed by many other explorers who wanted to trade with the Indians. They wanted furs, and the Indians wanted metal, guns, watches, beads, mirrors, and all the new things the explorers had. There was great excitement along the coast, and both European and Indian were eager to bargain with each other.

As more traders arrived, the Indian's way of life changed and Missionaries tried to convert them to the white man's religion. The Indians also moved closer to the new-comer's settlements to make trading easier, and soon found that the white man wanted the spoons, bowls, masks and other things that they had carved with such care — so they began to make more and more of them for trade.

Soon the new-comers wanted land to plant crops and build their homes on. At first they would give the Indian something in exchange for the land — but after a while they would just use it.

The white man's government made new laws and set aside lands for the Indian, called reserves. This is when the Indian way of life changed. He had to decide if he were to try to live as the white man did, or to continue in his own ways. His children had to attend schools which were often a long way from the reserves, and this split the family group. The children did not learn enough from the white man's schooling to live as they did, but began to question their Indian ways.

The new government did not allow them to hold their potlatches, so that there were few occasions for them to use their dances, songs, masks, robes and ceremonies. No longer could they show their wealth, or pass on their crests, titles and rights to hunting and fishing grounds in the manner that their tradition demanded. New laws governed fishing and hunting, and as the land became settled the wildlife gradually disappeared. Smallpox, a new and dreaded disease which the explorers brought, killed over half the Indian population. This resulted in such a rapid decline of their great culture that it was nearly lost.

Fortunately a few of the older people retained their skills and passed their knowledge on to the younger generation. Beautiful carvings in wood, silver and a soft stone called argillite are being made by Indian craftsmen today, and are in demand the world over.

**EAGLE — BASED ON
TLINGIT FRONTAL MASK**

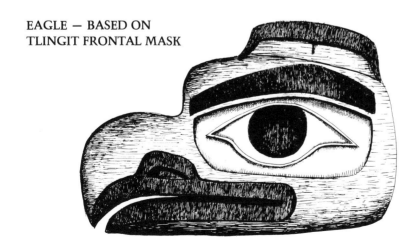

Index

Acknowledgements

I would like to express my appreciation for the assistance given by the staff of the Vancouver Centennial Museum, past and present, and the many other people knowledgable in this subject, who were most generous with their time.